LIFE OF THE BLESSED THEOTOKOS

Epiphanius Monachus

Translated by: D.P. Curtin

Dalcassian Publishing Company

PHILADELPHIA, PA

ISBN: 978-1-960069-62-7 (Paperback)

Library of Congress Control Number:
Author: Curtin, D.P. (1985-)

Front cover image: *Images of Thomas, Christ, and Simon Peter from Mosul*
Book design by J.J. Ripplestick

Printed by Ingram Content Group, 1 Ingram Blvd, La Vergne, Tennessee

First printing edition 2023.

3

Section I

De Maria , quæ proprie ac vere Deipara, et Semper-Virgo dicitur, multi e
vetustis doctoribus sermonem habuerunt: nam nonnulli quidem variis
propheticis figuris ac nominibus usi , mirabilia cum de ipsa, tum de eo , qui ex
ipsa ineffabiliter natus est, Christo vero Deo nostro prænuntiarunt: sancti
vero apostoli de Deo Verbo ex ipsa incarnato studiose egerunt, ac de iis quæ
ab ipso gesta sunt; de Maria vero cum pauca quædam dixissent, ad alia statim
transierunt, ita Spiritu sancto disponente . Sed omnes illam ex David originem
duxisse aiunt. Fuerunt autem c sanctis Patribus haud pauci, qui eam encomiis
celebrarent: sed ipsorum nullus de illius vita, et annis, aut educatione, aut
obitu, recte ac probabiliter scripsit. Imo qui id facere aliqua ex parte aggressi
sunt, a recta via aberrarunt, ac unusquisque sui ipsius veluti accusator exstitit,

ut exempli, gratia, Jacobus Hebræus, et Aphrodisianus Persa . Alli vero quidam postquam de Mariæ nativitate duntaxat locuti sunt, conti uo siluerunt . Joannes autem Thessalonicensis, qui de illius Dormitione celeberrimum scripsit sermonem, ipse semetipsum offuscavit, Alius insuper Joannes, qui Theologum se ipse denominat, mendacii reum se prodit. Andreas vero Hierosolymitanus, qui Cretæ episcopus fuit, postquam pauca quædam, eaque recte de hoc argumento dixit, encomium deinceps texuit potius quam narrationem. Nos vero cum plerosque examinaverimus , ac ea quæ credibilia, et firma, et vera essent cum ex Ecclesiastica Historia Eusebii, qui Pamphili cognominatur, tum e reliquis scriptoribus, ac magistris collegerimus, simplici nunc stylo cupidis lectoribus ea quæ ad Deiparam spectant exhibebimus: et cujusque scriptoris, e quo aliquid accepimus ne quis calumniari nos queat, quasi de nostro quidpiam addere, aut de- mere ausi simus, nomen in fronte indicavimus. Neque vero, si quid ex apocryphis libris, aut ex hæreticis deprompserimus, nos quis- quam redarguat inimicorum enim testimonia fide sunt digniora, ut Magnus ait Basilius. Quin etiam admirabilis vir Cyrillus Alexandriæ episcopus id ipsum fecit, ab Abrahamo usque ad David texens genealogiam Joseph, immaculate Deiparæ Mariæ sponsi ; deinceps vero etiam ipse, quoniam ex fratribus cum Josephus, tum Dei- para orta erat , ostendens sibi invicem non adversarii duos evangelistas , Matthæum nempe qui descendendo, el Lucam qui ascendendo ac retrocedendo genealogiam descripsit, in Nathan , qui et ipse fuit filius David, exorditur . Est autem rei demonstratio hujusmodi.

About Mary, who is properly and truly called Deipara[1], and the Ever-Virgin, and whom many of the ancient teachers had a discourse. They announced our God: indeed, the holy apostles acted diligently about God the Word from the very incarnation, and about those things that were done by him. Yet, when they had said a few things about Mary, they immediately passed on to other things, thus being disposed of the Holy Spirit. They all say that she derived her origin from David[2]. There were not a few of the holy Fathers who celebrated her with praises, but none of them wrote correctly and reliably about her life and years, or her education, or her death. Nay, those who attempted to do this in some part, strayed from the right way, and each one stood as his own accuser, as, for example, James the Hebrew, and Aphrodisianus the Persian[3]. Some of them, after they had just spoken of Mary's birth, fell silent. John of Thessalonica[4], who wrote the most famous sermon on his Dormition[5], has discredited himself. Andrew of Jerusalem[6], who was bishop of Crete, after saying a few things, and he said them correctly on this subject, afterwards weaved an encomium rather than a narrative. When we have examined most of them, and we have gathered from the Ecclesiastical History of Eusebius, who is known as Pamphilus, those things which were credible, true, and certain. As for the rest of the writers and teachers, we will now present to eager readers in a simple style those things which relate to Deipara. Of these writers, from whom we have received something, lest anyone should slander me, as if we had dared to add anything of our own, or that we had dared to do so, we have indicated the name in the front. Nor indeed, if we have reproved anything from apocryphal books, or from heretics, "let no one rebuke us, for the testimonies of our enemies are

---

[1] This is the Latin term for "Theotokos" or God-bearer. Since this translation employed the Latin text, the Western Catholic term is used here, despite its anachronism.

[2] That is to say, that she was a member of the House of David, as was a common tradition in the early church.

[3] He is said to have written a History of the Virgin Mary, however, very little is known about his life or the work itself, which does not appear to survive in any form.

[4] Presumably he is referring to John, the 7th century bishop of Thessalonica, although the exact sermon he is referencing is unclear.

[5] In the Western church the term that is used here is the 'Assumption' of the Virgin Mary.

more worthy of faith", as Basil the Great says. Moreover, the admirable man Cyril, bishop of Alexandria, did the same thing, weaving the genealogy of Joseph, immaculately married to Mary Deipara, from Abraham to David. Yet, afterward, since he had sprung from his brothers with Joseph, as well as the Deipara, showing that they were not in opposition to each other, the two evangelists, namely Matthew, who described the genealogy by descending, and Luke who described the genealogy by ascending and going back, in Nathan, who himself was the son of David. begins. Now there is a demonstration of this kind of thing.

Section II

Ex stirpe Nathan filii David oritur I: Levi autem genuit Melchi, et Pantherem. Melchi uxorem duxit, et filiis carens mortuus est. Panther genuit Barpantherem. Barpanther genuit Joacim patrem Deiparæ. E stirpe autem Salomonis, filii David, oritur Mathan. Hic generat Jacobum patrem Josuerui, et moritur. Tune Melchi frater Pantheris accipiens uxorem ejus, matrem Jacobi, genuit Eli. Itaque Jacobus fuit e stirpe Salomonis, Eli vero ex stirpe Nathan. Eli duxit uxorem, et mortuus est sine filiis ejus vero uxorem sumpsit illius frater uterinus Jacobus, et genuit Joseph. Josephus ergo natura quidem filius erat Jacobi; secundum legem vero erat filius Eli. Hi duo fratres unam eamdemque acceperunt in uxorem, quia les precipiebat, ut, si quis mortuus fuerit sine filiis, accipiat frater ejus uxorem ipsius, et suscitet semen fratri suo. Joacim, et Eli ex patre Panthere fratres erant: Eli, et Jacob ex patre Mathan erant fratres. Joacim genuit Mariam Deiparain; Eli vero genuit Josephum secundum legem: adeo ut Josephus el Maria essent filii fratrum. Josephus autem erat professione faber, et habuit fratrem ex Jacobo uterinum Cleopam, qui dicitur etiam Clopas.

---

[6] Also known as St. Andrew of Crete, the 8th century hymnographer.

From the line of Nathan the son of David comes 1: And Levi begat Melchi[7] and Panther[8]. He married Melchi, and died without children. Panther gave birth to Barpanther. Barpanther begat Joachim[9], the father of Deipar. And from the line of Solomon, the son of David, comes Mathan[10]. Here he begets Jacob, the father of Joshua[11], and dies. Melchi, the brother of Panther, took his wife, the mother of Jacob, and begat Eli[12]. And so Jacob was of the seed of Solomon, but Eli was of the seed of Nathan. Eli took a wife and died without his children, but his womb brother Jacob took a wife and begat Joseph. Joseph, then, was indeed the son of Jacob by nature, but according to the law he was the son of Eli. These two brothers took the same woman to wife, because the law commanded that if a man died without children, his brother should take his wife and raise up his brother's seed[13]. Joachim and Eli were brothers from the father of Panther. Eli and Jacob from the father of Mathan were brothers. Joachim begat Mary Deipara. Yet, Eli begat Joseph according to the law: so much so that Joseph and Mary were the children of brothers. Now Joseph was a carpenter by profession, and had a brother from Jacob's womb, Cleopas[14], who is also called Clopas[15].

---

[7] See Luke 3:24

[8] This name is highly controversial. In Talmudic literature it is the name given to Christ, "Bar-Pantera", with the pejorative point of reference being that a Roman Soldier named 'Pantera' was his biological father. The name itself is simply the Greek word for Panther, and not a proper name in itself. The 4th century Greek bishop, Epiphanius of Salamis claims that this was a surname to Jacob, son of Matthat.

[9] This name is regularly associated with the parentage of Mary, first appearing in the *Protoevangelium of James* in the second century.

[10] See Matt. 1:15

[11] This name does not appear in any other tradition regarding the Holy Family. This Joshua would therefore be the brother of Joseph the Carpenter.

[12] This tradition is taken from the writings of Sextus Julius Africanus, who claims that both men married an otherwise unknown woman named Astha (perhaps a variant of Esther).

[13] This is an attempt to synthesize the genealogical accounts rendered in the gospels, found in St. Matthew 1 and St. Luke 3.

[14] See Luke 24:18

[15] See John 19:25

Section III

Quoad maternum genus Deipara talis erat. Matham sacerdos Bethleemita habuit tres filias, Mariam, Sobem et Annam. Maria quidem pepe- rit Salomen obstetricem Sobe autem peperit matrem Joannis Baptista: Anna vero accepit Joacim fratrem patris Josephi. Et descendit Anna sponsa in Galilaam in urbem Nazareth: et habitavit Anna cum Joacimo annos L. quin filium gignerent. Factum est autem , ut ipsi ascenderent in Jerusalem in solemnitate Encæniorum: et dum Joacim orabat in templo, contigit , ut vocem audiret e cœlo dicentem ei: Tibi erit proles, et per eam glorificaberis. Concepit ergo ejus uxor Anna jam senex, et peperit filiam, et vocavit nomen illius Mariam, sororis suæ causa. Et congratulati sunt cum ea propinqui omnes atque amici.

As for the maternal race, the Deipara was this. Matham, a priest from Bethlehem, had three daughters, Mary, Sobe, and Anna. Mary indeed gave birth to Salome, the midwife, and Sobe gave birth to the mother of John the Baptist[16]. Yet, Anna took Joachim, the brother of Joseph's father[17]. And Anna, the bride, went down to Galilee, to the city of Nazareth, and Anna lived with Joachim for 50 years without having a son. And it came to pass that they themselves went up to Jerusalem in the solemnity of the Encenians[18], and while Joachim was praying in the temple, it happened that he heard a voice from heaven saying to him: 'You shall have children, and through her you shall be glorified.' Then his wife Anna, now an old woman, conceived and gave birth to a daughter, and called her name Mary, because of her sister. And all her relatives and friends congratulated her.

---

[16] That is to say Elizabeth

[17] This is taken from the identical account found in the fragments of Hippolytus of Thebes.

[18] That is a feast of consecration of a temple. In this case, the Jewish festival of dedication would be Hanukkah. Given the timeframe in question, it is estimated that this would have been around Kislev 25-Tebet 3, 3742, or in the Gregorian calendar December 11-18, 20 B.C.

Section IV

Cum tres jam annos nata esset puella Maria , duxerunt eam ipsius parentes in Jerusalem , et præsentarunt eam Domino cum muneribus. Et excepit illam, ipsiusque munera sacerdos Jodae qui Barachias quoque dicitur, Zachariæ pater. Et omnes sacerdotes gavisi sunt, et orantes benedixerunt Joacim, et Annam, et puellam Mariam. Hi vero abierunt in Nazareth. Cumque septennis facta est Maria, rursus parentes eam duxerunt in Jerusalem, et donaverunt earn Domino , consecra- tam ipsi per omnes dies vitæ suæ. Cumque hoc fecissent, paulo post Joacim pater ejus mortuus est annos natus, ut ferunt, octoginta, Maria B vero e templo non recedebat nec noclu, nec interdiu. Et Anna , relinquens Nazareth, venit in Jerusalem, et convivebat cum filia Maria: cumque supervixisset annos duos, mortua est annos nata septuaginta duos.

When the girl Mary was already three years old, her parents took her to Jerusalem and presented her to the Lord with gifts. And the priest of Judah, who is also called Berechiah, the father of Zechariah, received her, and her gifts. And all the priests rejoiced, and prayed and blessed Joachim and Anna, and the girl Mary. Thereafter, they went to Nazareth, and when Mary was seven years old, her parents again took her to Jerusalem and gave her a gift to the Lord, consecrating all the days of her life[19]. And when they had done this, a little after Joachim, her father died, aged eighty years[20]. Mary did not leave the temple, neither during the night nor during the day. And Anna, leaving Nazareth, came to Jerusalem, and lived with her daughter Mary. After she had survived two years, she died at the age of seventy-two[21].

---

[19] The *Protoevangelium of James* has this same event taking place, but at an earlier age.

[20] This would chronologically place the birth of Joachim around the year 93 BC, and his death about the year 13 BC.

[21] This would chronologically place the birth of Anna to be around the year 83 BC, and her death about the year 11 BC.

Section V

Maria autem parentibus orbata, qui ejus curam haberent, e templo Domini non exibat: ac, si qua re indigeret, ad Elisabeth tantum se conferebat: prope enim habitabat. Didicit vero Hebraicas litteras Joacimo patre suo adhuc vivo: oratque ingenio prædita, ac discendi cupida, et quamvis orphana, operam ac studium in divinas Scripturas conferebat: et in opificio lana, et lini, et serici, et byssi ob suam scientiam, at- que intelligentiam admirabilis erat plus quam aliæ omnes ejusdem ætatis adolescentule: adeo ut de ipsa illius proavus Salomon dixerit (revera enin de ipsa loquebatur): Mulierem fortem quis inveniet? et quæ sequuntur omnia.

But Mary, surrounded by her parents, who were taking care of her, did not go out of the Lord's temple, and if she needed anything, she only went to Elizabeth, for she lived nearby. She learned the Hebrew letters from her father Joachim while she was still alive. Her intelligence was more admirable than any other youth of the same age. So much so that Solomon, her great-grandfather, said of her (in truth, he was speaking of her): "Who shall find a strong woman?"[22] and all that follows.

Section VI

Erat autem in templo Domini locus segregatus prope porticum ex parte altaris. Ibi solæ virgines degebant et aliæ quidem virgines post dimissumn conventum ad suos cunctæ rever- tebantur: Maria vero manebat, custodiens san- cluarium, et templum, ac sacerdotibus ministrans. Ejus autem mores erant hujusmodi. Gravis atque augusta crat in omnibus actionibus, parum loquebatur, cito obediebat, alfabilis erat, modesta cum omnibus viris, risu abstinens et strepitu ac ira, libenter adorans, ad honorandum proclivis, et honorans ac venerans omnes viros, adeo ut universi ipsius intelligentiam, et sermonem admirarentur. Statura fuit mediocri: quidam tamen dicunt, fuisse plusquam mediocri. Triticei coloris erat, flavis crinibus, oculis flavis et

---

[22] See Ps. 31:10

pulchris, nigris superciliis, justo naso, longis manibus, longis digitis, longo vultu, diviuæ gratiæ, et speciei plena, fastus inimica, et complus, ornatusve, et mollitici; summopere humilis, ideoque eam respexit Deus, ut ipsanet ait, cum Dominum magnificaret, vestes amans, ac ferens nullo ascititio colore infectas, ut testimonio est sacrum ejus velum. Nebat autem lanas, cas nempe, quæ usui essent templo Domini, et alebatur ex templo Domini, operam constanter dans orationibus, et lectioni, et jejunio , et manuum labori, et cuilibet virtuti: adeo ut plerarumque mulierum magistra et operum varietate, et statu foret sanctissima Maria. Cum vero duodennis facta esset, contigit ut, quadam nocte dum oraret ad januas sanctuarii, media nocte lux splenderet solis splendore major: et vox e propitiatorio venit dicens ei: Paries Filium meum. Ipsa vero lacuit, nemini mysterium manifestans, donec in cœlum ascendit Christus.

———————

Now in the Lord's temple there was a separate place near the portico on the side of the altar. Only the virgins dwelt there, and indeed other virgins returned to their homes after the convent[23] had been dismissed. Mary, however, remained, guarding the sanctuary and the temple, and ministered to the priests. Her manners were of this kind: A pious queen in all her actions, she spoke little, was quick to obey, was able to speak, modest with all men, abstaining from laughter and noise and anger, willingly bowing down, inclined to honor, and honoring and reverencing all men, so much so that the intelligence of the universe itself, and they were surprised at the conversation. She was of average stature: some say, however, that she was more than average. She was of the color of wheat, with yellow hair, yellow and beautiful eyes, black eyebrows, a fair nose, long hands, long fingers, a long face, full of divine grace and appearance, an enemy's pride, and full, well-groomed, and supple; exceedingly humble, and therefore God looked upon her, as he said, when she magnified the Lord, loving clothes, and wearing clothes not infected with any color of ascites[24], as her sacred veil is a testimony. And she

---

[23] This might perhaps be anachronic in the Latin, as Judaism did not practice any form of monasticism at the time.

[24] It is unclear, but the author might be claiming that she utilized the now lost sacred color blue, Tekhelet (תְּכֵלֶת), which was intends to signify her rank and piety.

wove wool, that is, hair, which was to be used in the temple of the Lord, and she was fed from the temple of the Lord, giving constant attention to prayers, and to reading, and to fasting, and to the labor of her hands, and to every virtue: so much so that she was the teacher of most of the women, and of the variety of works, and of the state most holy Mary. But when she was twelve years old, it happened that, one night, while she was praying at the doors of the sanctuary, at midnight the light shone with the greater brightness of the sun: and a voice came from the mercy-seat, saying to her: 'Pray for my Son.' But she remained silent, revealing the mystery to no one, until Christ ascended into heaven.

Section VII

Abia vero princeps sacerdotum genuit Jodae , quem vocarunt Barachiam: hic vero genuit Aggæum et Zachariam, qui et ipsi sacerdoles fuere. Et accepit Zacharias consobrinam Mariæ, et rabitabant in Bethleem genuitque Joannem Baptistam. Aggæus autem Zachariæ frater genuit filian nomine Salome: eam accepit Josephus faber, alius Eli, et patruelis Mariæ et genuit ex ipsa sex filios, Jacobum, Simonem, Judam, Josen, Soben, Martham et Mariam. Et mortua est Salome uxor ejus, et Josephus viduitatem et continentiam servabat; annos enim natus erat circiter septuaginta, opibus pauper , arte faber , degens in Nazareth civitate Galilææ. Maria vero manebat in Jerusalem in domo Domini. Et cum facta esset annorum quatuordecim, qua ætate imbecillitas naturæ miliebris manifestatur, sacerdotes existimantes eam esse cæteris feminis similem (adhuc enim ignota erant mysteria ad illam spectantin), cousilio coacto, orationem pro illa fundebant.

Yet, Abijah[25], the chief priest, begat Judah, whom they called Barachiah, and he begat Haggai and Zachariah[26], who were themselves priests. And he took Mary's cousin Zachariah, and they traveled to Bethlehem[27] and gave birth to John the Baptist. And Haggai, the brother of Zachariah, begat a daughter named Salome: she was married to Joseph the Carpenter, another Eli, Mary's cousin[28], and by her he had six sons: James, Simon, Judah, Jose, Sobe[29], Martha, and Mary[30]. And Salome his wife died, and Joseph maintained widowhood and continence; for he was about seventy years old, poor in wealth, a carpenter by trade, living in Nazareth, a city of Galilee. But Mary remained in Jerusalem in the house of the Lord[31]. And when she was fourteen years old, at which age the infirmity of the gentle nature is manifested, the priests, thinking that she was like other women (for the mysteries concerning her were still unknown), forced her to pray for him.

---

[25] Abijah is here the ancestor of a division of priests. Jewish genealogies traditionally abridge their genealogies with the understanding that the missing generations are implicitly understood to be there.

[26] This account appears to be taken directly from the Chronicle of Hippolytus of Thebes *(Fragment I)*, where the brother of Zachariah is mentioned for the first time in Byzantine literature.

[27] Alternatively, tradition and the *Syriac Life of John the Baptist* places the town of Ein Karem in Judea as his birthplace.

[28] This "other Eli" is not mentioned in any other tradition, and it is unclear why it is mentioned here, as our author does not mention it again.

[29] This name appears frequently among the names of the family members of Christ. However, it is unknown elsewhere. It appears to be either a variant of the Hebrew 'Sabariah' or 'Sabar' (שְׂבַּר), or a corruption of the Greek 'Sophia' (σοφία).

[30] Despite utilizing Hippolytus of Thebes as a source, the name of Christ's sister appears different here. Hippolytus lists them as: Esther, Martha, and Salome. It is possible that Epiphanius is confusing the daughters of Joseph the Carpenter with the daughters of Mathan of Bethlehem, who are listed as: Sobe, Salome, and Anne.

Section VIII

Zacharias autem princeps sacerdotum, pater Joannis Baptista, sumpsit duodecim virgas a sacerdotibus consanguineis Virginis, easque posuit circum altare, dicens: Ostendet Dominus signo, cujusnam futura sit Virgo. Dum vero ili Orarent, germinavit virg Josephi fabri. Tum judicio Dei desponderunt ei Virginem Mariam non ad nuptias, sed ad custodiam et conservationem intemaratæ virginitatis: idque manifestum est ex ipsis verbis sanctæ Virginis angelo Gabrieli dieris: cum enim is ei post salutationem dixisset: Ecce concipies filium, et vocabis nomen ejus Jesum, et dabit ei Dominus Deus thronum David patris ejus, et cætera: respondit ei Virgo Quomodo fiet mihi istud, quoniam virum non cognosco? Nam si Josephus conjunctionis, et ccunubii lege eam despondisset, non ita ipsa respondisset, sed dixisset: Ex viro, cui nupta sum, aut desponsata, omnino concipiam. Sed cum sciret, quod is ipsam acceperat non connubii causa, sed ad eam custodiendam et conservandam, dixit ea verba veritatis plena: Quomodo fiet mihi istud, quoniam virum non cognosco? Non sum tradita viro nuptialis conjunctionis causa, sed ut perpetuo munda virgo et intacta servarer. Mujusmodi ergo fuit desponsationis causa.

———

And Zachariah, the high priest, the father of John the Baptist, took twelve rods from the priests who were related to the Virgin, and placed them around the altar, saying: The Lord will show by a sign whose future the Virgin will be. But while they were praying, Joseph the carpenter's vine sprouted[32]. Then, by the judgment of God, they espoused the Virgin Mary to him, not for marriage, but for the custody and preservation of her virginity[33]. This is evident from the very words of the holy Virgin to the angel Gabriel on the day, for when he had said to her after greeting her: "Behold, you shall

---

[31] The episodes being alluded to here is the one set out in the *Protoevangelium of James*, where Mary resides in the Jerusalem Temple complex until she is of marriageable age.
[32] A similar account is granted in the *Protoevangelium of James* IX
[33] This is not an uncommon arrangement in the ancient world, where marital relations are not necessarily venereal in their scope.

conceive a son, and you shall call his name Jesus, and The Lord God will give him the throne of David his father, and the rest." For if Joseph had betrothed her by the law of conjunction and consanguinity, she would not have answered in this way, but would have said: "I will conceive at all from the man to whom I am married, or betrothed." Yet, when he knew that he had taken her not for the sake of marriage, but to guard and preserve her, he said those words full of truth: "How shall this be done to me, since I do not know a man? I am not given over to a man for the sake of a marriage union, but to remain a perpetually chaste virgin and untouchable." The cause of the betrothal was of a different nature.

Section IX

Accepta autem Josephus patruele sua Maria e manu Domini, et omnium sacerdotum rei testium, deduxit eam in domum suam, et tradidit ei binas filias suas, ut eas quasi suas sapientia, et intelligentia instrueret. Ipsa autem degebat in domo Josephi cum omni humilitate, et gravitate. Cumque ibi mansisset sex menses, et de more jejuna foret circa horam nonam diei orante ipsa, revelatus est ei archangelus Gabriel missus a Deo el declaravit ei omnia mysteria de unigenito Filio Dei, quæ et in Evangeliis scripta sunt: ef nemo rescivit quod factum erat ex domo sua, nec ipsa id cuiquam annuntiavit, ne ipsi quidem Josepho, donec vidit in cœlos ascendentem Filium suum. Ideo dicit evangelista Matthaeus: Et non cognoscebat eam, donec peperit filium suum primo- genitum: hoc est: non cognoscebat mysteria Dei, nec absconditam profunditatem rerum, quæn ea perficiebantur. Erat autem dies hebdomadis prima: et juxta lunarem cyclum mensis primus, nempe Aprilis (hic est mensis primus in mensibus auni): dies prima ipsius, qua die primigenia tenebræ expulsæ sunt, dixitque Deus ; Fiat lux, et facta est lux: mensis autem sextus ab eo tempore, quo Joannes Baptista conceptus fuit: nam septimo mense Scenopegia, dum celebrarentur Encenia, et requies arcæ, Zacharias ingressus est in Sancta sanctorum solus, ul juxta legem suflimenta offerret, et apparuit ei angelus Gabriel. Ex eo tempore igitur numeran-tur menses, juxta lunarem cyclum: postea vero excogitatæ sunt indictiones ac meses Romani.

And when Joseph, her cousin, received Mary from the hand of the Lord, and all the priests were witnesses of the matter, he brought her into his house, and gave him his two daughters[34], so that she might instruct them in wisdom and intelligence. She dwelt in Joseph's house with all humility and grace. And when she had remained there six months, and was usually fasting about the ninth hour of the day, praying himself, the archangel Gabriel, sent by God, appeared to him and explained to him all the mysteries concerning the only begotten Son of God, which are also written in the Gospels. In her house this took place, and she did not announce it to anyone, not even to Joseph, until she saw her son ascending to heaven. That is why the evangelist Matthew says: "And he did not know her until she gave birth to her first-born son"[35]. That is, she did not know the mysteries of God, nor the hidden depth of things by which they were accomplished. Now it was the first day of the week and according to the lunar cycle the first month, namely April[36] (this is the first month in the months of the ram). The first day itself, on which day the first darkness was expelled, and God said: "Let there be light, and there was light" and it was the sixth month from the time when John the Baptist was conceived. In the seventh month, while the Scenopegia[37] was being celebrated, and the ark was resting[38]. Zachariah entered the Holy of Holies alone, who was to offer sustenance according to the law, and appeared the angel Gabriel to him. From that time, therefore, the months are counted according to the lunar cycle[39], but later the Roman indications and months were invented.

---

[34] This is perhaps confusing, as three daughters have previously been mentioned. It is perhaps assumed that an elder daughter has already been married, and is therefore not in the care of Mary as an active step-mother.

[35] See Matt. 1:25

[36] This roughly conforms to the Hebrew month of Nisan.

[37] The Jewish feast of Tabernacles, also known as Sukkot.

[38] Josephus indicated that the Ark of the Covenant was never in the Herodian Temple.

Section X

Quod vero ait sancta Virgo archangelo: Quomodo fiel mihi istud, quoniam virum non cognosco? sicut antea diximus, habet etiam quamdam aliam significationem, quæ aliena non est a prima nostra interpretatione superius tradita. Iloc est: Virum non concupisco: viri concup scentia careo: non novi voluntatem carnalis concupiscentiæ viri. Nec enim habebat virginitatem et continentiam cum tentatione, ut mulieres modestiores, ac de tenperantia sollicitæ, sed ex natura iliam habebat, quod eximium est ac singulare supra omnes feminas, et extraordinarium humanæ naturæ. Atque hoc illud est, quod ab Ezechiele propheta dictum fuit: Erit porta orientalis clausa, et nemo transibit per eam, nisi Dominus Deus Israelis: ipse solus ingredietur, et egredietur per eam: et erit porta clausa. Omnes insuper prophetæ et apostoli idem testantur: quin et ii qui sunt luminaria, et Patres nostri, et magistri catholicae et apostolicae Ecclesiæ hac in re consentiunt. Itaque magnus cliam Dionysius Areopagita de Christo ait: Supra hominem humana operabatur. Et virginali generationi testimonium perhibet etiam partus doloribus vacuus. Athanasius autem Alexandrinus, et Leo Romanus pontifex dixit de ipsa, quod concupiscentiam viri ignoravit. Et omnes sancta synodi orthodoxæ idem testantur. Ita Jacobus Hebreus, qui tunc aderat, et de illa scripsit, dicit: Cum fuisset singularis, et omnino extraordinarius partus, palpata ab obstetrice inventa est virgo ut ante partum et Rubim sacerdos id ipsum faciens per obstetricem, rei veritate convictus est. Quidam vero alii de hoc singulari miraculo dixerunt: Extraordinariam quamdam ren invenit natura. Alii autem: Supra fines naturæ fuit.

Yet, what did the holy Virgin say to the archangel: "How can this be done to me, since I do not know a man?" As we said before, it also has another meaning, which is not alien to our first interpretation noted above. The place is: "I do not lust after a man. I lack the lust of a man. I do not know the will of a man's carnal lust." For she had neither virginity, nor continence with temptation, as do more modest women who are concerned about

---

[39] The author appears to be familiar with the mechanics of the Jewish calendar, but

temperance, but she had it by nature. This was excellent and singular above all women, and extraordinary of human nature. This is what was said by the prophet Ezekiel: "The eastern gate will be closed, and no one will pass through it, except the Lord God of Israel."[40] He alone will enter and go out through it, and the gate will be closed. Moreover, all the prophets and apostles testify to the same thing: that even those who are luminaries, and our Fathers, and the teachers of the Catholic and Apostolic Church agree in this matter. And so the great writer Dionysius the Areopagite said of Christ: "He worked above man as a human being, and a virginal birth also bears witness to the absence of pain". Athanasius of Alexandria and Leo the Roman Pontiff, said of her that she was ignorant of the concupiscence of her husband. And all the holy orthodox synods bear witness to the same. Thus James the Hebrew, who was present at the time, and wrote about her, says: "When the delivery was singular, and altogether extraordinary, the midwife found a virgin palpated as before delivery, and Rubim, the priest doing the same thing through the midwife, was convinced of the truth of the matter". Some others, however, said of this singular miracle: "Nature has discovered a certain extraordinary thing". But others: "She was above the limits of nature."

Section XI

Sancta autem Virgo post apparitionem angeli statim abiit in Bethleem ad Elisabeth. Judæa vero, in qua civitas Bethleem sita est, excelsior est respectu Galilæ, in qua est Nazareth. Ideo ait Lucas: Maria autem cucurrit cum festinatione in montaṇam regionem, et ingressa est in domum Zachariæ, et salutavit Elisabeth. Ingressa vero cum esset, et eam salutavisset, notam fecit ei apparitionem angeli, et illius sermones, dixitque insuper ei, quod masculus erat is quem habebat in ventre, et quod Zacharias angelum viderat in templo, et ideo siluerat: quoniam Zacharias nihil locutus fuerat, noc enim poterat. Et ipsæ intra semetipsas mysterium tenuerunt, et nemini annuntiarunt serbrones ab ipsis factos. Et post tres menses descendit sancta Maria in domum Josephi. Erat autem composita et sermone , et moribus, et incessu sancta Virgo. Et

---

not with the specifics of it or the names of its months.

---

tempore progrediente, cum illius venter iutumesceret, Josephus videns sanctam, et ignorans mysteria ad illam spectantia, pudore perfusus voluit dimittere ipsam occulte e domo sua. Sed angelus Dei prohibuit quominus id faceret, sicut narrat Matthæus evangelista.

And the Holy Virgin, after the apparition of the angel, immediately went from Bethlehem to Elizabeth. But Judea, in which the city of Bethlehem is situated, is more elevated than Galilee, in which Nazareth is found. Therefore Luke says: "Mary ran with haste into the mountainous country, and entered the house of Zachariah, and greeted Elizabeth. But when she had come in, and had greeted her, he made known to her the apparition of the angel, and his words, and told her, moreover, that he whom she had in her womb was a male, and that Zachariah had seen an angel in the Temple, and therefore kept silent". For Zachariah had not spoken, as he could not. And they themselves kept the mystery to themselves, and announced to no one what they had done. And after three months St. Mary returned to Joseph's house. She was composed both in speech and in manners, in conduct of the holy Virgin. And as the time progressed, when her belly was full of pain, Joseph, seeing the sainted woman, and being ignorant of the mysteries pertaining to her, was filled with shame. He wished to send her secretly out of his house, but an angel of God prevented him from doing so, as Matthew the evangelist tells.

Section XII

Illo autem tempore contigit, ut descriptio fieret juxta Augusti Caesaris præceptum cendit Joseph e Galilæa in Judæam cum tota domo sua, ut describeretur juxta Cæsaris jussum: et filios quidem præmisit, filias autern, et sanctam Virginem Mariam sccum sumens cum jumento ascendit. Cumque in Jerusalem non pervenissent, in suburbano civitatis Bethleen, quod possidebat Salome consobrina sancta Deiparae, diversati sunt: et eadem nocte genuit

---

[40] See Ez. 44:1

Emmanuelem sancta Virgo, ministrante ad omnia Salome obstetrice, quæ erat in Bethleem, et erat ipsa quoque consobrina sanctæ Deiparæ Virginis Mariæ quoad maternum illius genus. Erat autem ibi spelunca, et stabulum quadrupedum. Cum vero ea quæ evenerant rescivit Elisabeth, attulit eis quæ usui futura erant, idemque fecerunt alii nonnulli consanguinei. Auditis autem iis, quæ pastoribus dicta fuerant, obstupuerunt. Et post biduum ex Persidis civitate Babylone veneruut Magi ab Oriente æstivo: viderant autem stellam a sinistro Hierosolymæ latere, talis enim est Persiæ situs respectu Judæ. Et stella non erat una ex aliis stellis, sed telluri vicina, et nunquam apparuerat, ut ait Joannes Chrysostomus. Et octavo die circumciderunt puerum, et vocarunt nomen ejus Jesum, hoc est, Salvatorem: et tunc reversi sunt in Nazareth. Descripti vero fuerunt Jacobus, et fratres ejus, qui erant filii Josephi: et descenderunt in Nazareth. Et completis XL diebus duxerunt puerum in Jerusalem, et obtulerunt eum Domino cum donis, et dederunt seni sacerdoti Simeoni: et benedixit eos. Et ibi divinitus monitus est Josephus, ut fugeret in Egyptum.

And in that time, it might be said that it was made according to the command of Augustus Caesar, Joseph went from Galilee into Judea with his whole household to be counted according to Caesar's command. And when they had not arrived at Jerusalem, they went their separate ways into the suburbs of the city of Bethlehem, which belonged to Salome, the holy cousin of Deipara, of Christ's mother's race. There was a cave there, and a four-footed stable, but when Elizabeth heard what had happened, she brought them things that were going to be used, and some other relatives did the same. When they heard what had been said to the shepherds, they were amazed. And after two days the Magi came from the Persian city of Babylon[41] from the summer east. They had seen a star on the left side of Jerusalem, for such is the position of Persia in relation to Judea. And the star was not one of the

---

[41] Magi could not have come from the city of Babylon, which had been abandoned for two centuries at this point. However, the region of Babylonia was under Parthian rule, and would not have been strange to have Zoroastrian astrologers present there.

other stars, but near the earth, having never appeared before, as John Chrysostom says. And on the eighth day they circumcised the child, and called his name 'Jesus', that is, the savior. Then they returned to Nazareth. James and his brothers, who were the sons of Joseph, were described, also went down to Nazareth. And when forty days were completed, they brought the child to Jerusalem, and presented him to the Lord with gifts, and gave him to the old priest Simeon, who blessed them. There Joseph was divinely warned to flee to Egypt.

Section XIII

Herodes autem diebus illis domesticum ipsius Salomes, Alexandro et Aristobulo: et cum uxorem interfecisset, perrexit Romam ad Cæsarem, et obtenta potestate reversus suffocavit etiam filios Salomes in fluvio, quasi deinceps oblivioni traditurus ea quæ dixerant Magi. Nactus vero tempus opportunum, et eorum recordatus, ira accensus est et post duos annos a Magis indicatos fecit Herodes infantium cædem. Et Zachariam, dum sacris operam daret, occiderunt milites intra sanctuarium. Elisabeth vero, quæ erat in Bethleem, Joannem sumpsit, et in desertum exivit, et dies xf latuit sub spelunca. Herodes autem post infanticidium se ipse gladio interfecit, annos natus LXX, Joannes vero ibi educatus mansit in desertis donec sese ostendit Israeli.

———

And in those days, Herod resided in the house of Salome[42], with Alexander and Aristobulus[43]. Thereafter, when he had killed his wife, he went to Rome to Caesar. Returning having obtained power, he also drowned Salome's children in the river, as if he was going to commit to oblivion what the Magi had said. When the opportune time came, he remembered them, and his

---

[42] It appears that our author is confused by the name of Herod's wife, called her Salome instead of Mariamne.

[43] The two sons of Herod the Great through his Jewish wife, the Hasmonean princess Mariamne. They were considerable political threats to him in their lifetime, as their claim to the throne was stronger than that of their father.

anger was kindled. After two years Herod, instructed by Magi, had the children slaughtered. Zachariah, while he was giving sacred service, was killed by the soldiers inside the sanctuary. Elizabeth, who was in Bethlehem, took John, and went out into the wilderness, and hid him under a cave for ten days. Herod, after the infanticide, killed himself with the sword at the age of seventy[44], while John, raised there, remained in the desert until he showed himself to Israel[45].

Section XIV

Et Josephus mansit in Egypto cum filiis A suis, et filiabus, et Deipara, et Christo anirus quinque: tum ob revelationem recessit, et reversus venit in Nazareth Galilææ. Et accepit filiam Mariam frater ipsorum Cleopas in uxorem suam. Cleopas autem frater ipsius Josephi ex eodem patre Jacobo nati. Et genuit ex ea Symeonem. Symeon vero iste post Jacobun fratrem Domini, episcopus fuit in Jerusalem: et sub Domitiano Romæ imperatore, post multa tormenta postea cruciaffixus est, annos natus 120, Jacobus autem filius Josephi, ut quidam dicunt, habuit uxorem duos annos, et illa mortua aliam non habuit. Judas vero frater ejus duos filios genuit, Zocerum et Jacobum ; sic enim vocati sunt. Ili astantes Domitiano imperatori Romae, ob eorum virtutem et sapientiam cessare fecerunt persecu- tionem Christianis illatam. Jacobus autem et Judas fratres Domini in numero sunt duodecim apostolorum. Joses vero et Symeon sumpserunt sibi uxores. Et Sobe convivebat cum Deipara continue. Joses autem a matre relictus est adhuc lactens, et enutrivit eum Maria filia Salomes consobrinæ Deiparæ.

Joseph remained in Egypt with his sons, his daughters, and Deipara, and Christ for five years. His brother Cleopas took his daughter Mary as his wife. Cleopas was the brother of Joseph himself, born of the same father Jacob.

---

[44] This did not happen. Herod died a slow painful death, but not of his own hand.
[45] See Luke 1:80

And by her he begat Simeon[46]. This Symeon, after James the Lord's brother, was bishop in Jerusalem, and under Domitian, emperor of Rome, he was afterwards crucified after many tortures, at the age of one hundred and twenty years. Judas, his brother, begat two sons, Zocerus and Jacob[47], for so they were called. They stood by Domitian, the emperor of Rome, and because of their courage and wisdom caused the persecution of the Christians to cease. James and Judas, the Lord's brothers, are among the twelve apostles. Joseph and Simeon took wives for themselves. Sobe lived with Deipara continuously. Joseph was left by his mother while still nursing[48], and Mary, the daughter of Salome, Deipar's cousin, nursed him[49].

Section XV

In solemnitate autem Paschatis reversi sunt ex Nazareth in Jerusalem , cum esset Jesus annorum decem. Cumque reversi forent in Jerusalem, a multis cognitus fuit, qui admirati sunt ejus intelligentiam, et sapientiam, adeo ut multos obstupefaceret. Erat autem valde pulcher aspectu, sicut Propheta ait. Speciosus forma pra filiis hominum: slatura longus erat sex pedes, flavis crinibus, pisto naso, flavis oculis, suaviter intuens, subflava barba, longis capillis: nunquam novacula ascendit in caput ejus, nec manus hominis, nisi matris ejus cum esset infans. Et cum fuit triginta annorum, baptizatus est a Joanne in Jordanis fline.

———————

On the solemnity of the Passover, they returned from Nazareth to Jerusalem, when Jesus was ten years old. When they had returned to Jerusalem, he was known by many, who marveled at his intelligence and wisdom, so much so that he astonished many. He was very handsome in appearance, as the

---

[46] Symeon of Jerusalem, who was said, according to Eusebius, to have died during the reign of the Emperor Trajan around the year 100 AD.
[47] These are in fact his grandsons according to Eusebius
[48] Presumably meaning that she died while he was an infant
[49] Because of the heavy repetition of the names Mary and Salome, it is unclear who this is supposed to be. The most likely candidate would be Mary, daughter of Joseph the Carpenter and Salome (his first wife).

Prophet says "A handsome figure before the sons of men"[50]. He was six feet tall, with golden brown hair, a pist nose, bright eyes, looking sweetly, with a tawny beard, and long hair[51]. A razor never went up to his head[52], nor a man's hand, except when he was a child of his mother. And when he was thirty years old, he was baptized by John on the banks of the Jordan.

Section XVI

Cum vero Joannes erat in deserto , annos 17. Ὁ natus et ipse triginta et unum (incipiendo nempe annum a mense Septembri) factus est ei sermo de baptismo; et venit in Judæam prædicans baptismum pœnitentiæ et remissionem peccatorum, et per baptismum etiam regnum cœlorum: non lamen etiam baptismum in Spiritu sancto. Et cum populi vidissent ejus vitam terribilem, atque admirabilem, secuti sunt eum multi, et facti sunt cjus discipuli. In his fuere et Andreas a Bethsaida urbe Galilæ, et Joannes a Zebeda. Principes autem sacerdotum cum audivissent quæ de Joanne promulgabantur, et de doctrina ejus, alii quidem, dicebant: llic est Christus; alii vero: Non est. Cum quæstio magna orta esset inter ipsos dehac re, miserunt ad Joannem, et interrogaverunt eum. Et dixit eis: Non sum Christus, sed pest me venit, medius autem inter vos stat. Factum est quadam die, ut essent multi populi et principes in deserto ad Jordanem apud Joannem confitentes peccata sua, et baptizati ab eo. Cumque Joannes populum doceret in Betharaca, qui locus est trans Jordanem, venit Jesus in desertum Jordanis, et mansit ibi dies 40, et rursus rediit ad Joannem. Ut autem vidit Joannes Jesum ad se venientem, ait de ipso: Eoce agnus Dei, qui tollit peccatum mundi: vidi enim Spiritum sanctum descendentem e colo, et manentem super eum, et vocem audivi dicentem ei: Hic est Filius meus dilectus. Et audierunt populi, et obstupuerunt. Postridie vero rursus vidit Joannes Jesum ambulanten, et ait de ipso: Ecce agnus Dei, qui tollit peccatum mundi.

---

[50] Possibly 1 Sam. 16:18
[51] Here is a rare physical description of the face of Christ. If this is true, he would have stood out in the Levantine hill country because of his height and eye-color.

When John was in the desert, at the age of seventeen, he was thirty-one (that is, starting the year from the month of September) and the discourse about baptism was made to him. and he came into Judea preaching the baptism of repentance and the remission of sins, and through baptism also the kingdom of heaven. I also do not lament the baptism in the Holy Spirit. When the people had seen his austere and wonderful life, many followed him and became his disciples. Among these were Andrew of Bethsaida, a city in Galilee, and John of Zebedee. When the chief priests had heard what was being proclaimed about John, and about his teaching, others indeed said: "Christ is there", but others said "It is not". When a great question had arisen among them about this matter, they sent it to John, and questioned him. And he said to them: "I am not the Christ, but a plague has come upon me, the middle stands between you." It happened on a certain day that there were many peoples and leaders in the desert at the Jordan near John confessing their sins and being baptized by him. And when John was teaching the people in Betharaca[53], which is a place across the Jordan. Jesus came into the desert of Jordan, and remained there for forty days, and returned again to John. When John saw Jesus coming to him, he said of him: "Behold, the Lamb of God, which taketh away the sin of the world."[54] And the people heard, and were amazed. But the next day John again saw Jesus walking, and said of him: "Behold the lamb of God, which taketh away the sin of the world."

Section XVII

Et audito hoc discipuli ejus Andreas et Joannes relicto illo secuti sunt Jesum, et venerunt cum eo in diversorium, et manserunt apud eum die illa. Quæsivit Andreas suum fratrem Simonem, et inventum duxit ad Jesum. Et cum audisset Jesus Joannem traditum fuisse , sequenti die exiit in Galilæam cum tribus discipulis. Et inveniens Philippum traxit eum, et is Nathanaelem: et venerunt in Canam Galilæ. Et post tres dies facta sunt nuptiæ, et vocati sunt:

---

[52] This would suggest the proposition that Christ had taken a Nazirite vow during his lifetime (Num. 6:1-21).
[53] This site is unknown, and is only mentioned in the writings of Epiphanius.
[54] See John 1:29

et Jesus ex aqua fecit vinum (nomen autem sponsi erat Simon, qui etiam post aliquot dies secutus est Jesum). Inde petiit Jesus Bethsaidam civitatem Galilæ, et ingressus est in domum Petri, et ægrotam hujus socrum superveniens sanavit. Cum rediissent in Nazareth, Josephus sponsus Deiparae mortuus est senex, et plenus dierum, annos natus, ut aiunt, centum et decem. Josephi vero filii Jacobus et Judas secuti sunt Jesum. Sed omnes simul ibant per urbes, et regiones, et prædicantes regnum Dei, et sanantes omnem morbum, et omnem languorem. Et socrus Petri sanata simul cum filia, uxore Petri, secuta est eos, et convivebat cum Deipara.

And when his disciples Andrew and John heard this, they left him and followed Jesus, and came with him to the inn, and stayed with him that day. Andrew sought his brother Simon, and found him and brought him to Jesus. And when Jesus had heard that John had been betrayed[55], the next day he went out into Galilee with three disciples. And finding Philip, he brought him forth, and also Nathanael. They came to Cana in Galilee. And after three days the wedding took place, and they were called. Jesus made wine from the water (the bridegroom's name was Simon[56], who even after some days followed Jesus). From there Jesus went to Bethsaida, a city of Galilee, and entered Peter's house, and coming up he healed his sick mother-in-law. When they had returned to Nazareth, Joseph, the husband of Deipara, died an old man[57], and full of days, aged one hundred and ten years. Joseph's sons James and Judas followed Jesus. They all went together through the cities and regions, and preaching the kingdom of God, and healing every disease and every infirmity. Peter's mother-in-law, being healed, followed them together with her daughter, Peter's wife, who lived with the Deipara.

---

[55] What this betrayal would be is unknown, as it is not recorded in any tradition regarding the life of John the Baptist.

[56] Simon of Cana, one of the twelve apostles, also known by the corruption of his name as Simon the Zealot or Simon the Canaanite.

[57] This account gives a similar age as the in the Coptic test '*The History of Joseph the Carpenter*'. However, that account notes that Joseph's death took place in Jesus' childhood, not during his ministry.

Section XVIII

Et inde discedentes, venerunt in castellum Bethsaidæ civitatis Galilææ, ubi est lacus qui Gennesareth, ac Phiala vocatur ob æqualitatem ambitus, et aquam omnino pellucidam ac mundam. Is habet septem milliaria in circuitu: oleum vero optimum est, et fructus autumnales circa lacum, et pisces bene olentes. Venit autem Jesus in Zebedam simul cum matre, et discipulis, et diversatus est apud Zebedæum, qui habebat uxorem, et duos filios Jacobum et Joannem, et accepit eos in discipulos. Mater illorum putans eun polliceri regnum terrenum, petiit ab eo, ut unus a dextris ipsius, et unus a sinistris sederet in regno ejus. Et inde egressi venerunt in Capernaum; et sanavit paralyticum, et alios multos. Ubicunque autem diversabantur, sponte illis afferebant inulta qui curabantur, et principes civitatum. Discipuli multos docebant, et baptizabant; Jesus vero non baptizabat, sed tantum docebat, et sanabat infirmos quocunque ibant. Zebedæus autem mortuus est: qua re audita Jacobus accedens ad Dominum ait: Sine, ut abeam ad sepeliendum patrem meum: et non pernisit ipsi. Et post breve tempus misit duos fratres Jacobum et Joannem bi vero abeuntes patrem quidem sepelierunt, matrem vero adduxerunt ad Christum et mansit cum Deipara reliquo vitæ ilaus tempore. Possessionibus vero suis venditis, quæ erant multæ, venerunt in Jerusalem, et emerunt Sion. Cum venisset autem Jesus simul cum matre, et ipsis discipulis in Judæam, et hi ubique Evangelium praedicarent, et baptizarent, et sanarent, ascenderunt in Jerusalem; et Salome uxor Chueze procuratoris Herodis Philippi habens septem spiritus nequitiæ accessit, et oravit Christum, et liberata est a spiritibus, et non reces- sit amplius a Domino, sed secuta est eum.

Leaving thereafter, they came to the fort of Bethsaida in the city of Galilee, where there is a lake called 'Gennesareth', also called 'Phiala'. Because of the equality of its surroundings, and the water being entirely transparent and clean. It is seven miles in circumference, and indeed the oil is excellent, and the fruits of the harvest surround the lake, as well as aromatic fish. Now Jesus came to Zebedee together with his mother and the disciples, and he stayed with Zebedee, who had a wife and two sons, James and John, and took them as disciples. Their mother, thinking that he was promised an earthly kingdom, asked him that one should sit on his right and one on his left in his kingdom. And leaving there they came to Capernaum; and he healed the paralytic, and many others. Wherever they went, those who cared for them, and the leaders of the states came to them of their own accord. The disciples taught and baptized many. Yet. Jesus did not baptize, but only taught and healed the sick wherever he went. When Zebedee died, and James heard of this matter, approaching the Lord, he said: "It is not so, that I may go to bury my father?[58]" He did not perish himself. And after a short time he sent two brothers, James and John, but when they went away they buried their father, but they brought their mother to Christ, and she remained with Deipara for the rest of her life. After having sold their possessions, which were many, they came to Jerusalem and brought them to Zion. When Jesus had come together with his mother and the disciples themselves into Judea, and they were everywhere preaching the Gospel, baptizing, and healing, they went up to Jerusalem. Salome, the wife of Chuza[59], the procurator of Herod Philip, having seven evil spirits. They came, and prayed to Christ, were freed from the spirits, and she no longer departed from the Lord, but followed him.

Section XIX

Cum vero ibi mansissent aliquot diebus (erat enim solemnitas Scenopegiæ), et multos doctrina illuminasset Christus, et e templo mercatores ejecisset, ac multos sanavisset a multis, variisque morbis, rediit in Galilæam, et venit in civitatem Magdala. Quædam mulier nomine Maria recepit eun in domum suam, et auditis sermonibus ejus, atque conspectis miraculis, quæ is faciebat, valedixit omni dorui suæ, accessit ad Christum, et sccuta est eum, et convivebat cum Deipara, et reliquis feminis. Erat autem prudentissima, et ferveus spiritu et lacrymis sicut Petrus, et de suis substantiis ministrabat eis. Discipuli autein erant Andreas, et Petrus fratres a Bethsaida civitate; Philippus et Bartholomæus, Jacobus et Judas fratres Domini (nam Joseph cognomento

---

[58] See Matt. 8:22
[59] Elsewhere he name is Joanna, and her husband worked for Herod Antipas, not Herod Philip (Luke 8:2-3)

dicebatur Alphaus); Simon a Cana, et Matthaus lista, Judas Hierosoymitanus, Thaddeus ab Edessa Syria, Judas proditor a Scara civitate, Jacobus et Joannes a Zebeda.

When they had remained there for several days (for it was the feast of Scenopegia[60]), and Christ had enlightened many with his teaching, and had driven out the money changers from the temple. He had healed many of various diseases, he returned to Galilee, and came to the city of Magdala. A certain woman named Mary received him into her house, and hearing his words, and seeing the miracles which he performed, she said goodbye to all her glory, and came to Christ. She embraced him, and lived with Deipara and the other women. She was very wise, and fervent in spirit and tears like Peter, and ministered to them of her own nature. The disciples were Andrew and Peter, brothers from the city of Bethsaida. Philip and Bartholomew, James and Judas, brothers of the Lord (for Joseph was called by the surname Alphaeus[61]), Simon ofCana, and Matthew the Publican, Judas of Jerusalem, Thaddeus from Edessa in Syria, Judas the betrayer from the city of Scara[62], James and John from Zebedee.

Section XX

Joannes autem Zebedæi fius, post mortem patris vendidit possessiones suas, quas habebat in Zebeda multas; et veniens in Jerusalem emit sanctam Sion, quæ est excelsior pars Hierosolymæ. Principes autem sacerdotum tunc singulis annis mutabautur, neque indigenæ erant, sed ex variis provinciis: unde et Caiphas a Cio provincia Bithynia, cum factus esset pontifex anm illius, morabatur in loco empto a Joanne Theologo: ideo dicitur fuisse notus Pontificis. Et ibi praeparaverunt Pascha, id est mysticain cœnam Christo eum discipulis et discipulabus. Cum autem ait: Ite ad quemdam, Joannem

---

[60] The Feast of Tabernacles, Sukkot
[61] This is inaccurate, Alpaeus if the Aramaic transliteration of the name Cleophas.
[62] The author here is alluded to St. Jerome's theory on the meaning of the name 'Iscariot', claiming that it was a city in Judea.

Theologum dicit, Ibi perfecerunt mysticam cœnam, et ibi manserunt post resurrectionem Domini. Cumque accepisset Joannes cruci astans a Jesu Matrem, duxit eam in domum suam, nempe in sanctam Sion. It ingree sus est Dominus januis clausis, et stetit in medio, et dixit: Pax vobis: et reliqua.

Section XXI

Unguentiferæ autem erant septem: Maria Magdalene, et Salome, et mater fliorum Zebedal, et Maria Jacobi Minoris mater, uxor Judæ fratris Domini, et mater Jose, quæ enutrivit fratrem Domini, et Joanna (hac, ut quidam dicunt, erat uxor Petri, ut vero alii aiunt, mater Clementis): et soror Matris Domini Maria Cleopæ, fratris Josephi: nam Joachim et Anna alium filium non genuerunt. Hæ unguentifere seplies noctu venerunt ad monumentum Domini, et quando surrexit, nescierunt. Deipara vero ad monumentum non ivit nocte illa; nam præ dolore jacebat. Sed dum angelus loquebatur cum Maria Magdalena, Christus apparuit in domo Theologi, id est in sancta Sion. Ibi manebant cuncti cum ipsa apostoli simul cum uxoribus, et cum Domini fratribus, jejunantes, humi cubantes, fentes, orantes et continue hymnos canentes magno cum gaudio. Ibi apparuit eis Christus sæpius. Missi ad varia loca et euntes, illic rursus congregabantur.

John, the son of Zebedee, after the death of his father, sold his possessions, which he had many in Zebedee; and coming to Jerusalem, he bought holy Zion, which is the highest part of Jerusalem. The princes of the priests at that time were changed every year, and were not natives to that city, but from various provinces. Also came Caiaphas, from the province of Bithynia[63], when he had become priest of it. He dwelt in a place bought by John the Theologian, therefore it is said that he was known to the priest. There they prepared the Passover, that is, the mystical supper for Christ, his disciples and apostles. And when he says: "Go to a certain place", he said to John the

---

[63] This is a region in Asia Minor, which seems unlikely. It is perhaps a corruption of Beth Anya, also known as Bethany in New Testament accounts.

Theologian, There they completed the mystical supper, and there they remained after the resurrection of the Lord. And when John, standing on the cross, received the Mother of Jesus, he led her to his house, that is, to holy Zion. The Lord entered the house with the doors closed, and stood in the midst, and said: "Peace be unto you, and the rest."

Section XXII

Videns autem sancta Deipara sui Fili Ascensionem in cœlos. multo magis se dedit exercitationi virtutum, et genuflexionibus; nam, ut ait Andreas Hierosolymitanus archiepiscopus Creta, usque ad hodiernum diem cavitates genuum ipsius in marmoribus sanctæ Sion osten duntur et situm reclinationis in lapide, ubi parum naturalis somni capiebat, prosequebantur honore et timore omnes homines, et glorificabatur non solum a fidelibus, sed a Judæis: et nullus Judæorum princeps, aut Græcorum audebat quid unquam de illa dicere, aut appropinquare domui, in qua ipsa manserat. Sion vero, et Gethsemani idem est. Multos autem infirmos sanabat, et obsessos a dæmonibus immundis liberabat: eleemosynas, et curam in pauperes, et viduas conferebat. Nullus vero e duodecim apostolis missus est, aut recessit ab ea quandiu ipsa vixit. Quin et in lapidatione protomartyris Stephant, quæ contigit septem annis post Christi Ascensionem, cuncti dispersi sunt præter illos duodecim. Et habebant Jacobumi fratrem Domini ut primum, et sine ipso nihil faciebant. Mulieres vero ex diversis provinciis nobiles cum Deipara erant, aliæ quidem a spiritibus immundis liberata, aliæ vero fidem amplexæ. Inter has erat etiam uxor Pauli , ut quidam dicunt.

———

Section XXIII

Hippolytus autem Thebanus narrat, eam vixisse annos omnino 59; nos vero invenimus eam diutius vixisse. Itaque prædictus Andreas episcopus Crelæ ex traditione ait, ipsam pervenisse ad magnam senectutem: at quinquaginta novem anni non faciunt magnam senectutem. Sed propter perturbationes nemo scripsit res illius; scilicet ob direptionem Hierosolymæ, quæ contigit viginti octo annis post Christi Ascensionem; et apostoli juxta angeli mandatum venerunt in civitatem nomine Pellam; sic enim ea vocatur. Dionysius vero Areopagita dicit se interfuisse dornitioni Deiparæ una cum Timotheo, et Hierotheo, et aliis. Hi autem erant discipuli Pauli: qui post sex annos, et dimidium baptizatus est, et post tres annos cœpit prædicare, et post novem annos discipulum habuit Dionysium! Ait autem beatus Paulus, se post viginti annos ascendisse in Jerusalem secundum revelationem 11; et invenimus in scholiis, cum ab Epheso raptus est Paulus, ob dormitionem Deipara raptum fuisse. Et cum dixit scribens ad Corinthios Apparuit ipsis plusquam quingentis fralibus simul 13 Christus post resurrectionem, de dormitione hoc dicit sanctæ Deiparæ.

––––––––––––

Hippolytus of Thebes tells us that she lived altogether fifty-nine years; but we find that she lived longer. And so the said Andrew, bishop of Crelæ, says from tradition, that she herself reached a great old age- fifty-nine years do not make a great old age. Because of the confusion, no one wrote down the matter; namely, because of the sacking of Jerusalem, which happened twenty-eight years after the Ascension of Christ[64]. The apostles, according to the command of the angel, came to a city called Pella[65], as it is called. Dionysius the Areopagite says that he was present at the burning of Deipar along with Timothy, and Hierotheus, and others. These were the disciples of Paul: who was baptized after six and a half years, and after three years began to preach, and after nine years had Dionysius as a disciple! The blessed Paul said that

––––––––––––

[64] This would be chronologically impossible, as it would place his ascension in the year 42. In likelihood thirty-eight would have been more reasonable.
[65] Eusebius claims that the early church took refuge in Pella during the First Roman-Jewish war.

after twenty years he ascended to Jerusalem according to Revelation 11. We find in the schools, when Paul escaped from Ephesus, that he was in audience with the Deipara, because she was asleep. When he wrote to the Corinthians, Christ appeared to more than five hundred brothers at the same time[66], thirteen after the resurrection, he says this about the sleep of the saints and of the Deipar.

Section XXIV

Monachus vero quidam presbyter virtute praeditus, et factis ac verbis pius, asseveravit dicens: Cum olim in his occupatus essem, quadam nocte, supervenit quidam dicens mihi: Apostolus Paulus ab Epheso in dormitione Deiparæ raptus fuit per nubem, et ascendit usque ad tertiam zonam stellarum, et inde vidit fines Oceani, et paradisum: cum vero audivisse arcana verba dicitur, hymni ab angelis et apostolis cantati designantur, quia duodecim apostoli per nubes advenerant. Sed mentitur. li enim qui ibi erant præsentes, Jacobus et Joannes, et Matthæus, quomodo per nubes venerunt? An forte, qui longe aberant? Dionysius qui ibi tunc aderat, hoc non dicit: neque ex duodecim illis antea mortuus quisquam fuerat, nisi Jacobus fratrer Joannis Theologi, occisus ab Herode, qui et Agrippa dicitur, filio primi Herodis ex Mariamne: qui etiam a vermibus consumptus fuit. Aliorum vero sanctorum, qui antea mortui erant , animæ omnes aderant.

A certain monk, a priest endowed with power and pious in deeds and words, saying: "When I was once occupied in these things, one night, a certain one came up". The apostle Paul from Ephesus was caught up by a cloud in his sleep by the Deipar, and ascended to the third zone of the stars, and there he saw the ends of the ocean, and paradise. When indeed he is said to have heard mysterious words, the hymn sung by the angels and the apostles is denoted because the twelve apostles had arrived through the clouds, but it is a lie. For those who were present there, James and John and Matthew, how did they

---

[66] See 1 Corn. 15:6

come through the clouds? Or perhaps those who were far away? Dionysius, who was there at the time, does not say this. Nor had any of those twelve died before, except James the brother of John the Theologian, who was killed by Herod Agrippa, the son of Herod the Great by Mariamne[67], who was also consumed by worms. But the souls of other saints who had previously died were all present.

Section XXV

Sancta vero Deipara quindecim ante diebus praedixit obitum suum : et tribus ante diebus venit angelus Gabriel, et significavit ei obitum et Domini praesentiam. Et ipsa misit ad invitandos apostolos omnes, et plerique venerunt ad illam: adeo ut fieret magnus, valde, et multus concursus. Exposuit ipsis tremenda mysteria, quæ in corde suo conservabat, et Salutationem angeli, et ejus visionem, et primam apparitionem, quam ipsa dum oraret in templo, vidit. Et testamentum fecit, ut ait sanctus Bartholomæus apostolus. Erat autem ipsa ob præteritas asceticæ vitæ perpessiones debilitata. Et cum venit hora ejus, Christus omnibus seipsuni manifestavit: et ob splendorem lucis omnes in terram ceciderunt præ timore, et facti sunt velut mortui; et dixit eis: Pax vobis. Omnesque præ gaudio convaluerunt. Et dum hymnos prius canerent angeli, homines stabant muti: deinceps hymnos cantarunt apostoli. Et ipsa velut dulciter dormiens, aperto ore, tradidit spiritum Filio, et Deo, annos 72. Et angeli lymnos rursus canentes abierunt. Sancti vero apostoli, ut dicit Dionysius Areopagita, qui aderat, cantarunt proprium lyinnum, non vero simul universi. Unde et hymnum Hierothei admirati sunt cuncti . El cantalis hymnis , post funebrem pompam posuc runt eam in monumento : nempe in Gethsemani. Et post parvum tempus , spectantibus omnibus qui aderant, corpus factum est invisibile ab oculis eorum. Et rursus canentes hymnos abierunt sin- guli ad proprias domos.

---

[67] These are his grandparents, and not parents. Herod Agrippa I's parents were the Prince Aristobulus IV and Bernice Costobarus.

The holy virgin foretold her death fifteen days before: and three days before the angel Gabriel came and signified to her the death and the presence of the Lord. She sent an invitation to all the apostles, and most of them came to her. So much so that there was a great, massive crowd. She explained to them the terrible mysteries which she kept in her heart, and the Salutation of the angel, his vision, and the first apparition which she saw while she was praying in the temple. She made a testament, as Saint Bartholomew the Apostle says. She herself was weakened by the sufferings of her past ascetic life. And when his hour came, Christ revealed himself to all: and because of the brightness of the light, they all fell to the ground for fear, and became as if they were dead. And he said to them: "Peace be with you." And they all recovered and rejoiced. And while the angels first sang the hymns, the people stood mute, afterwards the apostles sang the hymns. And she, as if sleeping sweetly, with her mouth open, gave up her spirit to her son, and to God, at the age of seventy-two. And the angels went away singing hymns again. The holy apostles, as Dionysius the Areopagite says[68], who was present, sang their own hymn, but not all together. Whence the hymn of Hierotheus[69] was sung in wonder. Canticles were sung, after the funeral parade they put her body in the tomb, there in Gethsemane[70]. And after a little time, in the sight of all who were present, the body became invisible from their eyes. And again, singing hymns, each one went to his own house.

Section XXVI

Anni vero ejus numerantur sic . Septenneni parentes eam Domino obtulerunt in Jerusalem. Mansit in templo sex annos , et dimidium: et in domo Josephi sex menses: tunc annuntiatum est ei gaudium totius mundi. Quinto decimo anno peperit. Et cum Filio fuit triginta tres aunos. Sunt simul anni 48. Post ascensionem Filii mansit in domo Joannis Theologi in sancta Sion simul cum ipso, et aliis qui ibi erant, annos 24. Summa est annorum 72. Post

---

[68] While this character is mentioned in Acts of the Apostles, there are considerable mystical pseudepigrapha composed by Peter the Iberian under this name.
[69] The first bishop of Athens

dormitionem vero sancta Deipara omnes apostoli dispersi sunt; et Joannes profectus est Ephesum. Matthæus autem evangelista dicit usque ad expugnationem Jerosolymæ nemo meo tempore missus fuit. Evangelium vero quod secundum ipsum est, post 30 annos scripsit ex mandato Jacobi fratris Domini, qui vixit , με dicit, post Ascensionem Domini annos 28. Jacobus autem iste partitus est ipsis regiones, et mittens eus, præcepit unicuique, ut singulis annis ei scriderent. quid docerent: quod et fecerunt, ut eorum doctrina consentanea esset prædicationi Christi, cui gloria et polentia in sæcula. Amen.

———————

Her years are numbered thus. When she was seven years old, her parents offered her to the Lord in Jerusalem. She remained in the temple for six years and a half, and in the house of Joseph for six months; then the joy of the whole world was announced to him. In the fifteenth year she gave birth[71]. And she was with her son for thirty-three years[72]. They are altogether for 48 years. After the ascension of her son, she stayed in the house of John the Theologian in holy Zion[73] together with him and the others who were there, 24 years. The total number of years is 72. After the sleep of the holy Deipara, all the apostles dispersed, and John went to Ephesus. Matthew the Evangelist says that until the conquest of Jerusalem no one was yet martyred. Yet, the gospel which is according to him, he wrote after thirty years at the command of James, the brother of the Lord, who lived, he tells us, twenty-eight years after the Ascension of the Lord. This James divided the regions among them, and sending him, ordered each one to write to him every year. They taught truly, so that their teaching was consistent with the preaching of Christ, to whom be glory and honor forever. Amen.

———————

[70] This appears to be the traditional tomb attributed to her in Jerusalem still found at the foot of the Mount of Olives.
[71] Roughly the year 5 BC
[72] Christ therefore would have left the house between 27-28 AD.
[73] That is to say, one of the mounts Jerusalem is built upon.

www.ingramcontent.com/pod-product-compliance
Lightning Source LLC
Chambersburg PA
CBHW061104050726
47592CB00004B/1817